# PRELUDE TO BLACK SATURDAY

### A Play
### For Good Friday

## C. Alton Robertson

CSS Publishing Company, Inc., Lima, Ohio

PRELUDE TO BLACK SATURDAY

ISBN: 0-7880-0732-7                                      PRINTED IN U.S.A.

This work is dedicated to
all those faithful believers who
throughout the centuries have
kept the faith alive.

# PREFACE

This play is written especially for Good Friday and should begin at 12 noon. The actors should be in their places, sitting in silence, as the congregation enters.

The cast includes

        5 — Soldiers
        6 — Jews
        4 — Women
        2 — Thieves
       11—Disciples
        1 — His mother
        1 — The Christ

Speeches shown as ALL and those indicated for a whole group are to be delivered as a Greek chorus by the group indicated.

The setting: Three crosses are at the front of the sanctuary. The men on the crosses face the front of the chancel with their backs to the congregation. The other actors face the crosses and the congregation.

# FOREWORD

Following a Good Friday service many years ago, a friend expressed disappointment to me because, and I paraphrase her words, "When I leave a Good Friday service, I want to know that he is dead. I don't want any hint of Easter and the resurrection."

What today is Holy Saturday on the Church's calendar was certainly not Holy Saturday for those early followers of Jesus. It was a day of despair, truly a Black Saturday.

This play came to me virtually as a whole. Once I began to write, I did not stop until the first draft of the drama was completed. It became obvious to me that the words and desires of my friend had become my own, and in my unconscious I had devised a Good Friday service that might capture the reality of that Friday when my Lord was crucified.

C. Alton Robertson
Redlands, California
Lent, 1995

# PRELUDE TO BLACK SATURDAY

**THE JEWS:**

ALL — "The King of the Jews." Ho, King!
    King on a cross.
King on a wooden stick of a throne.
    King. King. King. Ha!

I — Tear down this temple. Destroy it.
    And, in three days, I will build it again?
That's a nice joke, Prophet.
    A funny, funny joke.

ALL — A nice joke.
    A funny joke.
A nice, funny joke.

II — Save yourself.
    Come down and prove your claims,
You, Son of God!
    Ho!

**THE CHRIST:**

"Father, forgive them. They know not what they
do."

**THE MOTHER:**

My son, my son.
    My firstborn.

Is this why I birthed you?
>For this end did I suffer disgrace
And accusations,
>Pointing fingers and whispers?

Is this the throne of David
>That Gabriel promised?

Is this to rule over the house of Jacob?

Is this the bitter end of bitter herbs
>Drunk in innocence in response to a blinding
>vision?

Born in a barn
>And killed on a cross.
A rude end
>For a rude beginning.

A bed of straw for a red, new baby.
>A crown of thorns for a sunburned man.

My prince of peace,
>My eldest son,
Son of God Almighty,
>What meaning has this death?

**THE SOLDIERS:**

I — He's the one all the noise was about last Sunday.

II — And the noise today, too.

III — But different noises, these.
>The harmony of praise dying
In the clashing, clanging commotion
>Of convictionless crowds.

8

IV — He's from Galilee, they say.
     Only three years ago, he began to preach.

V — A healer, they say.  A worker of miracles.
     A speaker with authority unlike men.

I — One said that Herod's slaughter of the innocents
     in Bethlehem
    Was caused by the predictions
     at his birth.

ALL — And this morning, Herod's son
     Scoffed at him and jeered.
    Scoffed at him and jeered.

II — Let us divide his clothes
     And get this over with.

## THE DISCIPLES:

ALL — Is this the end?
     Is this the bloody end
    Of all our expectations?

I — Master, is this the Way?

ALL — Why?
     Were you not the Christ?

II — What meaning has this?
     Why?

    We warned you before we came.
     We tried to stop you.

    But you have been silent.
     Silent.  Silent.

III — You were not guilty of those accusations.
    Yet you did not deny them.

IV — You are letting this happen.
    Letting it happen.
Letting it happen.

ALL — And you are silent.
    Silent. Silent.

**THE THIEVES:**

I — Your disciples are confused, Carpenter.
    They didn't expect this end.
As you gasp and die on this stick,
    You shatter all their dreams of grandeur.

Carried in on the wave of your popular appeal,
    They expected cabinet posts
And praise and honor.

But this kind of treatment
    Is not what they bargained for.
The fools.
    The poor, sick fools,
Living on the hope put out
    By a carpenter.

You really knew how to take them in
    With false hopes, didn't you?

Speak to them, you fake.
    Stick it to them.
Admit that you're a phony.
    Let them in on what suckers they were
And what a hopeless pickle they're in now.
    Confess what a liar you've been.

II — Be silent, you idiot.
   Are you blind?
  Can you not see that this man is not one of us?
   You and I,
  We deserve this death.
   We stole and lied and profaned.
  We ignored society and its laws.
   We knew the consequences of our acts
  If caught.

  This man has done no wrong.
   Obviously, he has given, not stolen.
  He has spoken truth, not lied.
   He has suffered for society, not made it suffer.

I — I blind?
   Nonsense.
  You've been taken in
   Like those simpering women down there.

  The sun and pain have clouded your mind.
   In your state of half-awareness,
  You view this Carpenter King and you're deceived.
   Die quickly, you fool,
  And get it over with.

II — Die.  Yes, die.
   And in quiet oblivion rot.

  Yet can it be that …
   Can it be?

  You, Jesus, remember me when you come
   Into your kingdom.
  Remember me.
   Remember me, please.

11

**THE CHRIST:**
> "This day shalt thou be with me in
> Paradise."

**THE WOMEN:**
ALL — Take her home.
> Take her home.
> She mustn't stay here longer.

> Return, Mary.
> > Return and weep.
> Return and pray.
> > Return.
> Return and forget.

I — Our Christ hangs upon a cross.

II — I dream. I dream.
> This nightmare can't be true.

III — The perfume had meaning
> Beyond my intention.
> Why couldn't it have been more?
> Yet why did it have to be
> The spice of death as well as the
> Fragrance of gratitude?

ALL — John, support his mother
> Before she faints.

> The strain is great.
> The burden impossibly heavy.
> Those nails pierce her, too;
> And her heart,
> Like her hands and feet,
> Feels their tear
> And rough and rusty presence.

| IV | — | How could such a one be crucified? |
|---|---|---|
| I | — | Has the world inverted? |
| II | — | Has all that was true become false? |
| III | — | Has wrong become right? |
| IV | — | Has the total universe eclipsed? |

ALL — The sun. The sun.
      It grows so strange.

I — The rumbling.

ALL — The rumbling.

II — The very earth protests this crime.

ALL — She weeps again.
      She weeps.

**THE CHRIST:**
      "Woman, behold thy son.
      Son, behold thy mother."

**THE WOMEN:**
ALL — Oh, Mary, do not wait here.
      John, take her home.
      Guard her.

III — Shield her.

IV — Protect her.

I — To see the fruit of one's womb devoured
      Is misery.

ALL   —   Misery.

II   —   Is misery.

ALL   —   Misery.

        Shield her.
          Shield her.

**THE JEWS:**

        The sun has disappeared.
          The rumbling increases.

**THE SOLDIERS:**

        The wind begins.

**THE WOMEN:**

        The groan and travail of a universe bent in pain.

**THE DISCIPLES:**

I   —   What deformed child is being born?

II   —   What warped and maimed shape
          Will emerge
    From this rape?

III   —   Into the void of this noontime night …

ALL   —   Into the void of this noontime night …

**THE WOMEN:**

        This noontime night …

**THE JEWS:**

        Noontime night …

**THE DISCIPLES:**

III   —   Into the void of this noontime night,
          What monster comes?

IV   —   He was the Light.

ALL   —   But now all light is gone.

      For a brief moment
          Humankind's eternal night saw dawn;
      But, before the sun could emerge,
          Humans, in fear, have pulled the curtain.

      The Day is ended.
          And Night is re-entered.

**WOMAN IV:**

      The hope of Life has turned to despair.

**DISCIPLE VI:**

      The apple has been devoured
          By the worm.

**DISCIPLE VII:**

      Evil laughs.

**THE WOMEN AND THE DISCIPLES:**

      Evil laughs.

**DISCIPLE VII:**

      Evil laughs
          The hollow laugh
      Of hollow victory.

      And existence,
          Which may have taken meaning
      Had this life continued,
          Now reverts to daily struggle

For survival
Lived out in insignificant moments
Dedicated to meaninglessness
And making sheer existence a folly.

**DISCIPLE VIII:**
Can there be a God above
When things like this take place?

**THE WOMEN AND THE DISCIPLES:**
Can there be a
God above?

**DISCIPLE IX:**
Can there be a God of justice ruling
When justice dies?

**THE WOMEN AND THE DISCIPLES:**
When justice dies.

**THE DISCIPLES:**
ALL — Deluded by an ancient myth
Our parents perpetuated,
We sought to find a God
That
Today has shown conclusively
Is nonexistent.

X — Against the civil law of Rome we struggled
Because a greater law of Yahweh stood
Above the state.
Yet civil law,
Urged on by religious men,
Now kills Yahweh's son;
And Yahweh is silent.

**THE WOMEN:**
> The son himself is silent.

**DISCIPLE X:**
>> Beneath the civil law of Rome
>>> We now must live
>> With the dreadful knowledge that
>>> Until a stronger civil law arises,
>> There is nothing greater
>>> and nothing—
>> Nothing can be done.

**THE SOLDIERS:**
> *(Matter of factly)* Nothing can be done.

**THE JEWS:**
> *(As if correcting the disciples)* There is  nothing
> **you** can do.

**DISCIPLE XI:**
>> Earthbound life
>>> Today is bound more completely
>> To the earth than ever before.
>>
>> Cords that Abraham sought to loose
>>> And Moses tried to cut,
>> Today pull tightly around all persons
>>> And, in the binding,
>> Kill the very thought that
>>> Freedom from them is a possibility.

**THE DISCIPLES:**
>> Earth's animals shall no longer dream
>>> Of being something more than
>> Time and Space contain.

**THE SOLDIERS:**
>Earth's animals shall
>>No longer dream
>
>The silly dream
>>Of being something more than
>
>Time and Space contain.

**THE DISCIPLES:**

ALL — Today, the Temple is destroyed.
>Today, the faith of ages past

Dissolves,

I — Evaporates,

II — Disintegrates,

III — Disappears.

ALL — The darkness of the Godless night
>Enfolds us all,

And humankind withdraws into the
>Vacuum of non-meaning

And non-non.

**THE WOMEN:**
>The darkness of a Godless night . . .
>>The darkness of a Godless night
>
>Enfolds us all.

**THE SOLDIERS:** *(The beginning of a luring, coaxing attempt to sell a belief. Spoken softly.)*

I — Give yourselves to the dark.
>You are its children.

II — Be obedient to your parent, Night.
>Kick not against the wall of dark.

**THIEF I:**
>Do not struggle with the inevitable.
>>Accept the truth of this day.
>In resignation, accept the facts of life.
>>Yield to the night of death.

**THE SOLDIERS AND THIEF I:**
>Yield to the night of death,
>>The supremacy of Evil,
>The ultimacy of meaninglessness.

>Accept this.  Do not struggle.
>>Yield.  Do not resist.
>Give up.  Relax into the folds
>>Of darkness and sleep.

**THE SOLDIERS:**

I   —   Release your dreams.

II   —   Throw off the unreality
>That has falsely sustained you.

III   —   Join your master.
>In submission, receive your fate.

ALL  —  Go into the Night
>And lie in peace.
Submit, embrace,
>And sleep.

**THE CHRIST:**
>"My God, my God, why hast thou forsaken me?"

*An interlude of quietness and darkness*

**THE CHRIST:**
>"I thirst."

**THE JEWS:**
ALL   —   What's this?
              Does he call Elijah?

I     —   I'll bring a sponge filled with wine.

ALL   —   Wait.

II    —   Let this be a test.
              Will Elijah come?

ALL   —   Will Elijah come?

**THE WOMEN:**
              Will Elijah come?

**THE DISCIPLES:**
              Will Elijah come?

**THE JEWS:**
III   —   If this be a prophet of God,
              Then thirst should be no problem.

ALL   —   The parched, burned King,
              With ripped hands
         And feet deformed,
              Through lips
         Chapped and split and bleeding,
              Calls for liquid,
         Experiences thirst.

**THE SOLDIERS:**
I     —   It is just a man we kill today.

ALL   —   It is just a man.

I   —   A strange, dreaming laborer
               Who has caused a ripple
           In a little pond.

           A stone too small
               In a pond too insignificant
           To ever affect the Sea.

ALL   —   Write out the report.

II   —   Write out the report in triplicate.
               Forward one to Pilate.
           Send one directly to Rome
               And file the third.

           Three men we kill today.
               Three men.  Nine forms.

ALL   —   Three men.  Nine forms.
               Today's work.

III   —   Tomorrow's memory.

ALL   —   The next week's forgotten fact.

**THE JEWS**:
           No one has come.
               Give him the sponge.

**THE DISCIPLES:**
ALL   —   No one has come.
               Give him the sponge.

           The eternal well has gone dry.

III   —   If it ever existed at all.

ALL  —  The spring of life
          Trickles to a stop.

          The Way leads into
            A cul-de-sac
          Where we circle ourselves.
            A dead-end
          Demanding our retreat.

IV  —  I'm going fishing. *(Leaves.)*

*An interlude of quietness and darkness*

**THE CHRIST:**
          "It is finished."

**THE SOLDIERS:**
          Finished.
            The job is done.

**THE WOMEN:**
          Finished?
            Finished?
          Can it be?
            How can it be?
          The end.

**THE DISCIPLES:**
          It is finished.
            It … is … finished.
          The dreary climax of a strange third act.

          The author is a cynic.
            This is the end.
          It is finished.

22

**THE JEWS:**
>It is finished!

**THE MOTHER:**
>Is it finished?

>"And you shall call his name Jesus,
>>For he will save his people from their sins."

>"Do you not know that I must be
>>About my Father's business?"

>"Who is my mother and who are my brothers?
>>Those who hear the word of God and do it,
>These are my mother and my brothers."

>"He who loves father and mother more than me
>>Is not worthy of me."

>"If you would be my disciples,
>>You must take up your cross daily
>And follow after me."

>Is it finished?

>It is finished.

>Let us go.

*Quietness and darkness as ALL but the WOMEN depart*

**THE CHRIST:**
>>"Father, into thy hands I commit my spirit."

*(The soft weeping of women is heard.)*

The congregation leaves in silence.